C000255909

THE DIET AND
AN AMAZONIAN

Laurent FONTAINE

&

Fermín RODRÍGUEZ YUCUNA

ISBN 978-1-7398937-7-4

Design and production by John Hunt at mapperou@gmail.com

Callender Press I Milton Keynes, UK

callenderpress.co.uk I hearingothersvoices.org

THE DIET AND PATH OF
AN AMAZONIAN SHAMAN

Laurent FONTAINE

&

Fermín RODRÍGUEZ YUCUNA

CALLENDER NATURE SERIES 4

CONTENTS

INTRODUCTION

When I went to Colombia for the first time in 1997, I had in mind to learn as much as I could from the knowledge accumulated over millennia by the last shamans of the Amazon that I could meet. Not to lose their tremendous unexplored heritage of knowledge for me was one of the greatest challenges of the 21st century. But I did not imagine how urgent the task was in the Amazon, not only because of the disappearance of the last authentic healers, but also because of the lack of new apprentices.

After having spent more than a month visiting the Yucuna communities alongside the banks of Lower Caqueta and Miriti-Parana, between La Pedrera and Jariyé Boarding School, I was desperate to never meet one of these authentic healers that I had come to seek. To my great surprise, it was only once returned to the village of La Pedrera that several so-called "shamans" came to me. But there was no need to inquire further to discover that in such a village, any Indian quite fond of the drink and knowing three words of incantation could claim to be "shaman". Many of them are nicknamed *El Brujo* or *Payé* ("The shaman").

My despair stopped when I met Mario Matapi, a nice sexagenarian recently moved from Jariyé, who boasted not only of knowing the mythology like the back of his hand, but having learned most of the incantations and ceremonial songs in two years. I only wanted to see, but I got stung by an ant Paraponera just below the gigantic millennium cockspur coral tree that borders the river (Photo 1). My ankle was so swollen that I had to lie and put my foot up for a whole week. During the four days I spent at the health center, Mario came to see me several times. On his second visit, he reassured me that I was going to recover quickly. The night before, he had made an incantation for me and he applied a little coca on my ankle which completely deflated in two days.

In the Tanimuca community of Comeyafu in front of La Pedrera on the other side of the river, Mario invited me to the little house on stilts temporarily lent by one of his (classificatory) "brothers" or patrilineal cousins. He had come to live there with his wife Elvira Yucuna, and his two-year-old granddaughter he was taking care of, while the mother was working in Leticia.

Then it began for me the research I had been dreaming for years. Every night, while I was dozing in the darkness with my tape recorder turned on, Mario liked to tell me the longest myths with more details than those recorded 25 years earlier by Pierre-Yves Jacopin, my thesis supervisor in anthropology (Jacopin, 1981, 1988 ; Fontaine, 2013). And when I finally went to bed around midnight, Mario was still awake the second part of the night pronouncing long incantations sometimes until dawn.

Mario is not a Yucuna, but a Matapi (or *Jupichiya*). Like three other descent groups: the Je'rúriwa, the *Jimíke'pi* and the *Jurumi,* the Matapi lost their original language during intertribal conflicts and ended up speaking the language of their allies Yucuna (self-identifying *Kamejeya*). When I asked Mario to tell me a list of yucuna speaking healers, he gave me only a few names that he counted on the fingers of one hand. He reported that the Yucuna lost their last shamans because of the measles outbreaks that had occurred during the Colombo-Peruvian War of 1930-1933. But thanks to the Macuna, two Je'rúriwa have now become renowned shamans. The first is Pedro Rodriguez. He left the region to settle in Villavicencio as a "traditional surgeon", but he transmitted his shamanism to one of his *je'rúriwa* nephews, Fermín Rodríguez, who is also Mario's favorite son-in-law (Photo 5). In Yucuna, such shamans are called *lawichú* (or *brujo* in Spanish), they are generally considered as the most powerful, because they would be able to "see" and "extract" diseases of the body, and even to travel in the form of jaguar. Outside of these shamans, Mario said there were only a few healers left. Old Bonifacio[1] and himself were the only ones who still remembered a large repertoire of Matapi incantations.

---

[1] Bonifacio Matapi (also called *Mawi*) died in 2004. He was the informant of Pierre-Yves Jacopin who recorded with him some myths and incantations.

The last other Yucuna-speaking language trainer recommended by Mario was the old Milciades, a "real Yucuna" (Kamejeya), who still knew how to make blowguns, and who lived near the end of the La Pedrera airstrip (Photo 2).

Thereafter, I also met Milciades (Photo 6) and every time I stayed in La Pedrera, I went to work alternately at his house and at Mario's. But for that, it was first necessary to familiarize myself with the Yucuna language for years, both through mythology and conversations, before being able to grasp the intricacies of their shamanic language. Finally it was very worthwhile because each time I came back to do fieldwork, I could grasp and appropriate a little more of the immense knowledge held by these two elders. Every day, they seemed to me a little more like cultural treasures alone. Learning their language allowed me to communicate better and better with these living encyclopaedias of unsuspected knowledge. And every day I discovered a little more than an inexhaustible mass of fascinating and useful knowledge on all fauna and flora.

But what impressed me the most about these healers was not so much the extent of their knowledge, it was mostly the effectiveness of their knowledge in terms of the powers they give them, especially with regard to memorization, divination, healing, clairvoyance, communication and distance action. I was always amazed to hear them daily quickly reciting masses of knowledge in long incantations lasting up to 20 hours even though they were illiterate (Fontaine, 2011, 2013, 2014, 2015, 2016). I wondered how they could have acquired so much knowledge without writing, by unknown methods, radically different from those of the school or the university.

In the shamanism, there are always two ways: the first occurs unexpectedly while the second is voluntarily taken by the subject. In the first case, he has not made any decision; he has simply been chosen by an invisible entity (spirit or master of the forest, ancestor) who has come to meet him suddenly. This happens most often in altered states of consciousness that occur during a traumatic event (illness, accident) in which the person escapes from death or sees his soul momentarily projected into the universe of spirits. The Yucuna tell the adventures of Malawichure, their greatest shaman, having increased his powers tenfold during visits to the spirits of the underworld. This happened recently to a Tanimuca lost in the forest and starving. Some say he was "eaten" and "replaced" by the spirit of a forest mistress, while others consider that he was simply taught by an invisible entity.

In the second case, the subject expresses his will to develop his powers with master shamans to practice initiation rituals that will allow him to acquire or regain the powers of his ancestors[2]. For anyone who, like me, has never had the opportunity to be called by supernatural entities, the second way is more interesting since it not only allows you to go and ask them for a particular spiritual development, but also to recover shamanic powers long since lost by his ancestors. This is not done without a certain commitment at least equivalent to that which an elected official must make.

Fermín, Mario's son-in-law, had taken exactly that way that interested me. In 2003, he moved to Camaritagua shortly after his father-in-law, the community that adjoins the village of La Pedrera. He had helped him to build a maloca (traditional roundhouse, see Photo 3) and prepare the rites of foundation. Like Mario and Milciades, Fermín was angry with members of the Jariyé community. His uncle Pedro Je'rúriwa, who had taught him shamanism, had been the first to abandon Jariyé for the same reasons. He even confided to me in 1999 that he personally punished the community of Jariyé by casting a spell on it so that it would be deserted by all its medicine men. Anyway, the misfortune of this distant community of Miriti-Parana made me happy, since less than a kilometer walk from the airstrip of La Pedrera, I could work with the three best yucuna speaking medicine men of the region.

---

[2] There are several types of motivation that can drive some people to meet such an entity, such as the quest for knowledge, the craving for power, the desire to become exceptional and to be respected as such, the desire to acquire exceptional faculties, or the need to benefit others.

The first time I saw Fermín, it was during a second stay in Jariyé that I had worked with Milciades in December 1998. While many members of the community had come to watch a game of micro-football on the cemented ground that adjoins the Internat, Milciades had told me: "It's him, Fermín the shaman." He was a man of about 33 years old, who looked much younger with his hair cut in brush, observer and silent. He had never spoken to me. But I had then met for the first time his father Arturo (Photo 6), who was also a healer, certainly less famous than Milciades and Mario.

While working with Mario in his maloca in Camaritagua, Arturo and Fermín often came to see me. With Arturo, I recorded myths, and two of his other sons transcribed them for me. As for Fermín, he had chosen to teach me *The story of the first Je'rúriwa*,[3] as well as the "shamanic truths" that he personally experienced or observed as a shaman. He regreted that too few young people are interested in shamanism and most of them remain ignorant or careless about the countless invisible dangers of this world. In his teachings, he started by describing to me *The masters of the plagues* (2006) which crack down each period of the year, and against which it is advisable to know how to protect oneself. Then he told me *The Path of the Souls* (2008) explaining what happens after death according to the acts committed on this earth. Having had little schooling, he always dictates to his wife Virgelina in Yucuna language what he wants to transcribe (Photo 4). But Fermín can represent more or less abstractly his shamanic visions in iconic or graphic forms, whether in wooden sculpture (seat, Photo 7), weaving and basketry (palm leaf roofing, Photo 8 ; calabash holder, Photo 9), engraving (maracas, Photo 10), traditional painting (masks, Photos 11 and 12) or in drawing, as the illustrations in this book show.

---

[3] Cf. Rodríguez Yucuna Fermín, 2008.

Photo 1. *Millennium cockspur coral tree in the village of La Pedrera.*
Photo 2. *Airplane view of the La Pedrera airstrip.*
Photo 3. *Mario Matapi's Maloca near La Pedrera (2003-08).*
Photo 4. *Fermín and his wife Virgelina (2003-09).*
Photo 5. *Mario Matapi and his son-in-law (2004-10).*
Photo 6. *Milciades Yucuna, his son and Arturo(2002-08).*
Photo 7. *Jeta'pá (Yuc.). Traditional seat.*

Photo 8 · Photo 9 · Photo 10 · Photo 12

Photo 8. *Different weaving patterns of palm leaf roofing.*

Photo 9. *Jumichirípuku (Yuc.). Hyperboloid calabash holder.*

Photo 10. *La'rí (Yuc.). Maracas.*

Photo 11. *Mureru (Yuc.). "Eared mask" of the Peach Palm Ceremony.*

Photo 12. *Muñecos del baile de chontaduro (Span.). Disguised dancers of the Peach Palm Ceremony.*

Photo 13. *Pupa (Yuc.). Walking palm (Socratea exorrhiza), where are made the largest Yurupari flutes and trumpets.*

Photo 11

Photo 13

LEARNING SHAMANISM

Let us come to the path that Fermín had resolutely followed to become a shaman. After several years of working with him, he once revealed to me how this path permitted him to regain the power of his own ancestors although it seemed definitively lost as for most other indigenous peoples today.

The recovery of ancestral power

Formerly our elders enjoyed the power of their ancestors, like all the tribes who inherited the shamanism. But that disappears today, because the young generations are no longer interested in it. Some ethnic groups, however, like the Macuna and the Yauna still master the words of their ancestors, even if they also lose them little by little. The ancestors of the Matapi also had the power of their ancestors, but they lost their shamans long time ago. Their ancestors themselves caused this loss. This is why the Matapi can no longer receive the charge of being shaman. The only tasks they can take on are the chants, the incantations, the roundhouses and the rites of Yurupari[4]. As for the Yucuna (Kamejeya), they also received the words of their ancestors, but by dint of cursing each other, their shamanism[5] was also lost not so long ago[6]. All that remains is the dancing ceremonies and the roundhouses. Nowadays, very few of them really know things. This is the end of their knowledge.

---

[4] As mentioned above, Bonifacio and Mario Matapi are not shamans, but healers (or more precisely "incantators", specialists of incantations).

[5] **Marichú kaje** (Yuc.). shamanism. Here Fermín speaks of shamanism in its most noble sense, that is to say reserved only for shamans worthy of the name (*lawichú*) who can "see" and "travel" in different worlds, unlike the healers (*lawichú ra'runa*).

[6] According to our informants, the last great yucuna (*kamejeya*) shamans died from the measles epidemics spread during the mobilization of the Indians in the Colombo-Peruvian war (1930-1933), notably to Araracuara to build an airstrip.

Similarly for the Je'rúriwa ancestors. It has been a long time since our shamanism was lost. Nevertheless, it is thanks to the Yucuna that we still know something. They are the ones who gave us back the power of vision of our ancestors, the incantations of Yurupari and roundhouses. As they shared with us these things, they can say that it is thanks to them that we benefit from them.

Memorization of myths and small incantations

How was it possible to recover knowledge and powers lost for generations? What were the conditions necessary to reclaim them? What do these conditions presuppose as shamanic principles?

> However, if some say we do not have shamanic knowledge, it's because they do not know our story. Indeed, our ancestors have received this shamanism; they fasted or went on the diet as well. And the Yucuna made us inherit the visionary power of our ancestors. If they had not gone on the diet, we would not have been able to receive such power. We would be without anything today.
> Some time ago, our ancestors lost the shamanism. But after that, we were able to relearn the visionary shamanism of our ancestors thanks to the Macuna. If we could learn the words of our ancestors, it is thanks to their incantations. And that requires a diet, otherwise we die quickly.
> By means of incantations, it is necessary to begin by treating the child with a decoction of genipa for washing him of all the impure things he has eaten, before putting him on a diet. Afterwards, we do stronger incantations so that he quickly retains the myths, the shamanic words, etc. During the first year, he has to listen to the myths, then the first small incantations, for instance to cure the bullet ant stings.

To better understand the lessons of this experience, let us summarize its conditions and principles. Fermín mentioned four *basic conditions* for all learning of a young male.

These conditions are also required to pass the Yurupari rituals that will acquire a new adult name and new teachings to assume a traditional status (leader, singer-dancer, healer).

It is obligatory:
– *To have been purified.* This is done by an incantation and a bath of genipa juice.
– *To fast or being subjected to a diet.*
– *To have received incantations facilitating the memorization.*
– *To learn myths and small incantations.*

Several principles are presupposed[7]:
– *The genipa has a purifying property* (Principle 1).
– *Fasting and diet increase memory* (Principle 2).
– *Incantations have effects on entities* (Principle 3). For example, there are incantations to facilitate the learning of a young person, to release the active potential of a natural substance such as the genipa, and to cure the bullet ant stings.

Lana Ra'a rinaku

FAN'A RA'A RINALU
RINAJAKO LOJE PENAJE

Kuya chu lana

Tincture of genipa (yuc. lana) is put on the body of the young man to make him pass the tests of Yurupari.

---

[7] These presupposed principles are very general, and others will be encountered later. They apply implicitly in many speeches, practices and rites of the Yucuna. It is therefore appropriate to number them in parentheses, in order to be able to indicate each of them precisely if we find them elsewhere, in particular in this book.

The first tests of Yurupari

> After the first year, he has to do more serious incantations to
> reorder the world (to prevent disaster), and to prepare the
> Yurupari ritual. From there, he is put on even more diet, and is
> isolated from his parents and his brothers. He can't even go see
> them anymore. He is then subjected to severe tests to be able to
> see the Yurupari. And the tests must be repeated. At this point,
> the incantations are really very serious.

As learning becomes more serious, the trials are more numerous
and difficult for all the young men who have to pass the Yurupari
rituals to perfect their learning. Yurupari is the Ancestor shaman
Trainer, under whose authority young men are taught.

The story of Yurupari Ancestor is partly told in the last episode of
the myth of the Four Karipú's Grandsons who, according to the
Yucuna, created this earth. They went to get the Yurupari to give
the rituals of initiation to men. But in the early days, many men
died while consuming forbidden foods. Then the Karipú's
Grandsons burned the Yurupari. But he was reborn from his ashes
with his brothers and his sister in the form of walking palm
(*Socratea exorrhiza*, Photo 13), bamboo, several species of trees
and a liana. Thanks to various animals, the Karipú's Grandsons
gradually learned to use them to make sacred large horns whose
sound is the voice of their minds. Since then, it is these horns that
still allow new generations of men today to practice initiation.

To be considered as initiated in Yurupari, four conditions are
required:

- *a severe diet, away from hot foods, oily flesh and fruits;*
- *an isolation from parents, brothers, children and women;*
- *a treatment with incantations to pass the Yurupari;*
- *repeated tests of Yurupari.*

In Yucuna language, to undergo the tests of Yurupari is called *wajákaje* which also means "to punish", "to chastise", "to flog". The Yucuna consider that it is by testing the mind that it can be disciplined to acquire knowledge. Throughout the Yurupari ritual (between 3 and 6 days), young men have:

– *sleep deprivation* (no more than two hours of sleep per night),
– *overnight immersion* by spending several hours each night lying in the river,
– *obligations to vomit many times daily in the forest.*

When they are not disciplined enough, or when they slightly disrespect the diet, they have to compete with endurance and courage by forcing them *to whip each other*, and to *absorb pepper juice through the nostrils.*

Young men practice vomiting and absorb pepper juice through their nostrils.

Ask and assume the charge of shamanism

> We then ask him:
> – What do you want to be in charge of? Dancing ceremonies, cure, shamanism?
> Sometimes there are the parents who say what they want their son to become:
> – I want you to be shaman, my son.
> One does the incantations so that he could be shaman. The diet is even stricter.

As stated in the introduction, the first requirement for initiating the path of shamanism is *to ask to assume this charge to a shaman instructor*. This may very well be imposed on the applicant by his parents, but he will have to accept it, by certain words at crucial moments, as we shall see.

The request to the Jaguar Ancestor

> (As shaman trainer) one informs the Jaguar Ancestor. To visit such ancestors, one must carry in spiritual form of some coca, some tobacco snuff and a cigar. Arriving in their house, one says:
> Here I am, grandfather. I brought you some coca, some tobacco snuff and a cigar. One gives them, and says:
> – I have come so that you may give me the shaman's power.
> The Jaguar Ancestor answers:
> – What you came for requires a diet. It is not safe. It can kill you very quickly. But since you came for that, we'll tell you what you're asking for. What are you going to take? Look well, grandson.
> So we look, and we see beautiful things hanging around in the roundhouse. There are clubs, seats, magical jaguar mantles, jaguar mirrors, lightning instruments, gloves to remove diseases, jaguar-tooth necklaces, calabash holders, calabashes, cigars, clubs adorned with eagle feathers. The splendor of these things illuminates the whole roundhouse.

The Jaguar Ancestor answers:

– What do you come for, grandson? What is next to the back door is really not a game, the diet is severe to control this. Rather, I advise what is next to the main pillar. But it is still dangerous. Not everyone can support the diet. Without diet, it is impossible to control it. What is next to the main entrance requires a lot less diet. But it does not have much shamanic power. What do you want to ask? It is then we must evaluate the level of diet which is capable to take on the boy. The request must be adapted to his capacity. And one replies:

– That's what I want, grandfather.

– Good, said the Jaguar Ancestor. The latter takes a cigar and blows tobacco smoke on the chosen shamanic instrument. And something falls in the middle of the roundhouse.

– This is the power of the ancients. I advise you, because you came looking for this for our grandson that you are preparing, recommend him to follow the diet well. Otherwise he would soon die before having completed his training. The novice must be isolated because of what he has requested. At the end of his training, we will leave him this power. Then one takes this shamanic power. And one brings him back here to give him this power of jaguar.

The second condition to initiate the path of shamanism is *the request of the instructor to the Grand Ancestor Jaguar*. Fermín does not explain here how this is done. But he once told me that shamans could "travel in dreams". Healers usually pronounce their incantations with their eyes closed in the darkness, then they enter a modified consciousness that is close enough to waking dream or self-hypnosis. This dream trip is always perceived as a separation of the soul from the body that is designated in the West by the terms "astral travel" or "out-of-body experience". This soul travel would allow them to visualize such encounters. But such a visit cannot be empty-handed. To go see a Grand Ancestor, you *must always prepare him coca and tobacco to inhale*.

For any healer, this type of offering is done simply *by imagining sharing with the ancestors of these substances each time they consume them.* On the one hand, they help him to go into ecstasy to visualize the ancestors. On the other hand, as they dry up faster than he thinks he has absorbed himself, he deduces that the ancestors used them in an invisible way.

The placement of shamanic elements in the body of the apprentice

One says:
– Come here, little boy. This is when the Yurupari is going to do around the roundhouse, during the trial of initiation. Then, the young man receives the mantle and the mirror of jaguar, the power to throw lightning, the gloves to extract the diseases. All this is placed in his body in a spiritual form. It is invisible.

This arrangement of shamanic elements in the body of the apprentice is always done by naming each of them (with all the ancestors who are the masters) in incantations (Fontaine, 2016). To begin learning shamanism, the young man *must receive shamanic elements in his body through an incantation of his instructor during a Yurupari ritual.* These then make him particularly "delicate" or "fragile". This is why it is necessary for him to follow a very long and severe diet.

Years of diet

The young man must obey his strict diet. And he must also accept all the Yurupari ritual. When one treats the foods that can be eaten again by people who have passed the ritual, the apprentice must continue his diet for a full year. He must undergo a special diet that will allow him to consume only small fish, cassava bread, manioc beer, manioc sauce during the same year. With this diet, he can eat neither anything hot or which has been touched by a woman, nor go where a woman having the period, nor let her approach him.

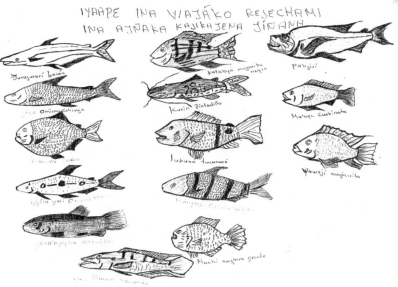

IYAAPE INA VIAJÁKO REJECHAMI
INA AJÑAKA KAJIKAJENA JIÑANA

*Fish banned from consumption for young Yurupari practitioners
as long as they have not spent at least twice.*

He can't eat smoked food, salty, or weevil larvae. Not either smoked white-lipped peccary, smoked armadillo, capuchin monkeys or toucans. Forbidden fish such as fat fish (*Brycon erythropterum, Brycon melanopterus, Mylossoma* sp.), several tetras (*Characidae*), big catfish (*Paulicea luetkeni, Brachyplatystoma filamentosum, Leiarius* sp.), etc. Not either animals producing stomach aches such as tufted capuchin, woolly monkey, paca, two-toed sloth, greater long-nosed armadillos, yellow-footed tortoise, twist-necked turtle, arrau turtle, Geoffroy's side-necked turtle, matamata turtle, coati, howler monkey, tamandua, giant anteater, etc. The novice must have his own saucepan that no one touches. So is the diet to learn shamanism. If he eats hot, he experiences hot flashes and nausea. If he eats food prepared by a woman, he exposes himself to diseases. His body heats up, he loses his mind and forgets what he has learned. If a woman having her period comes close to him, he is in grave danger. Her heat affects him by causing the confusion of his mind.

It makes his jaguar mantle dirty, and deteriorates his jaguar mirror. When we tell him the myths, he does not retain fast. His mind mixes up everything. And he passes out.

If he eats smoked food, he is also in danger. His ears are clogged, as if they were covered with clay pots. He doesn't hear well. If he eats salty food, his jaguar mantle becomes dirty. He can't quickly remember the shamanic words. If he eats *mumú* weevil larva, it is very serious. He can't touch it or smell it. If he touches or eats it, the forest masters kill him with one of their arrow, in the form of a snake. Having eaten a forbidden food, he can also be killed by the Yurupari at once. Also, it is difficult to vomit weevil larvae during the Yurupari ritual. Likewise with the *wawaru* weevil larva. If he eats it, his body heats up, and his jaguar mirror becomes dirty. He will no longer see well. The weevil larva clogs his ears with the sawdust of its galleries. In addition to becoming deaf, his teeth will also get worse. Because the weevil's teeth have the spirit of lightning. That's why it was born with a jaguar mantle[8]. If he eats freshly smoked white-lipped peccary, the Yurupari will want to kill him, and if it is not him, it will be one of the arrows of a forest master. If he eats armadillo, the forest masters will also kill him. He can also die of a tumor. Or one of his feet could be rotten. If he eats tufted capuchin or touches its meat, the Yurupari and the forest masters want to kill him. Even with a recently smoked toucan, the Yurupari or a *pá'yumi* (master of the water) want to seize him. With forbidden fish recently smoked, the forest masters and the Yurupari want to kill him. And if he eats animals producing stomach aches[9], he will suffer badly with it. He can't swallow any fruits from the gardens. Cane sugar spoils the teeth, bananas give worms that affect the stomach and cause diarrhea, as well as yams. The abiu fruit[10] is the spirit of a woman (of an invisible world), that's why we can't eat it. As well as the avocado, if he eats it, the jaguar mantle is lost.

---

[8] This weevil has a spotted yellow aspect reminiscent of that of the jaguar.

[9] **Ojina** (Yuc.). Category of animals that, without protective treatment, it is better to avoid consuming, because their meat would cause upset stomachs such as "ulcers" or "gastritis".

Animal masters of upset stomach (yuc. ojina)

If he sleeps with a woman, he loses his own mind, because it falls into the underground world[11]. The woman's spirit sucks[12] it like a soft-fleshed food. The jaguar mantle gets lost, then it goes back to its masters. He finds himself without anything. From illness to illness, he ends up dying. That's why he has to follow the recommendations; otherwise while we believe to do well, we prepare his own death. There are also the wild fruits: sylvan abiu, abiu of the woodland, *Pouteria ucuqui*, *Oenocarpus bataua*, sylvan inga, *açaí* palm, calabashes, etc.

---

[10] **Jima** (Yuc.). *Caimo* (Span.). *Pouteria caimito*. Abiu is the appearance in our world of what is a woman in another world.

[11] The spirit of an apprentice shaman has the shape of a tasty food in another world, which is why, if it is exposed, it can be eaten.

[12] **Apiro'kaje** (Yuc.). *Chupar* (Span.). Absorb without chewing, so without necessarily needing teeth. For example: eat soft-fleshed fruits such as abiu, guamo, uva, bananas, etc.

Yurupari said:
– If you swallow one, I'll suck your mind like you did with one of these wild berries.
In the eyes of Yurupari, the spirit of the culprit becomes a fruit, he enjoys it. However, you can eat field mouse, gray brocket, collared peccary, collared titi. And also some birds: marbled wood quail, undulated tinamou, great tinamou, grey-winged trumpeter, cinereous tinamou. So must be the diet for a year. The young man learns the myths, small incantations, how the forest masters appeared, and how their weapons look like.

As for any young person passing the Yurupari ritual, the apprentice must be subjected to numerous dietary and sexual prohibitions. But in his case, these do not last only the time of the ritual, they must continue during all the years necessary for the development of the shamanic elements placed in his body.

Dietary and sexual restriction is *to prohibit direct or indirect contact with women, high-fat animal flesh, stomach-rotting animals, soft-fleshed sweet fruits, salt and heat sources.*

How to explain the presupposed commonalities of all these prohibitions?

According to several explanations collected from Fermín and other healers, several sensory contacts (kinaesthesic, gustatory, olfactory and visual) are proscribed with all the elements that can be connected or assimilated to a female genital tract. Indeed, the Yucuna shamanism must always be kept away from any gestation, from any feminine procreation that nourishes or carries life. The shamanic development goes even in the opposite direction, since it is always as close as possible to the ancestors' spirits. *Only foods that are "cold" or associated with masculinity* (Principle 4), such as those based on cassava, or certain small fish with low caloric value, are allowed.

Prohibited animals that can not be eaten recently smoked.

The apprentice cannot come in contact (even indirect) with a woman or her period, nor consume any hot food, get close to a fire, or expose himself to the sun.

On the contrary, if it must extend every night in the river, it is because *its shamanic elements can grow only by being kept in freshness* (Principle 5).

For the apprentice, *any sensory contact with a hot or greasy element deteriorates his body as well as the shamanic elements placed there* (Principle 6).

Fish, weevil larvae, white-winged peccaries, sapajous and other animals characterized by their fatty flesh are considered even more dangerous. In the spirit world, some predator spirits like Yurupari or the water master Pá'yumi can detect such fats in the body of the apprentice who has consumed them and jump on him to delight and swallow his soul. Any fat is also reminiscent of a woman well fleshy and fertile.

It is the same for many fruits, prohibited for the roundness of their forms and the sweetness of their flesh, which allows to consider them as "the women of Yurupari".

From this we deduce the following principle:

Any apprentice who comes into contact with the flesh of a woman, animal or fat or sweet fruit becomes irresistibly attractive to predator spirits, who will not miss any opportunity to engulf his soul (Principle 7).

The first tests of the apprentice

After a year, the elders make new incantations to reorder the world and prepare another Yurupari ritual. The novice must still be tested to verify if he respected his diet and all the recommendations. One looks through his body to see how the shamanic elements that he received are. If they are not dirty, and if his spiritual power is developing in his body, one says: "It's good". And the Yurupari is happy because he has been obeyed.

By contrast, if the young man violates the recommendations, the jaguar mantle which was offered to him is all stained and in bad condition. The spiritual power of the novice becomes puny. Then he is told:

– We can't do anything for you now. You didn't obey us. You have damaged the shamanic power that was placed in you. When one sees that he has not respected the recommendations, one must remove all from him that we had laced in him by means of incantation. Without which, he could get sick and die. Because the Yurupari is furious, he wants to kill him. That's why we must remove all this power from him. He finds himself without anything, without knowledge. He must follow the diet in his own interest, to gain the power of the elders.

Then we continue to pass the Yurupari ritual and to do the incantations for the young man. And we go on telling the myths until he finishes all his rites of Yurupari. After each of these rituals, we treat the food that the young men will be able

The elders gather to reorder the world before a new Yurupari ritual.

to eat again. As for the young man who has received the shamanic power, he will have to continue his diet.

And after a new year, we do new incantations to re-arrange the world again and we make a new Yurupari ritual. We still look at the young man to see if the shamanic elements placed in his body are developing normally. And if that is the case, we are satisfied. He has respected his diet. And the Yurupari is happy too. One then teaches him the important incantations until the end of the ritual. Once the Yurupari is gone, the food of those who have passed the ritual is treated again.

It is then that we can begin to treat the aspiring shaman with salt so that he can eat gradually a little salty and hot. So that he can go out in full sun, or light cigars and cigarettes. A new year passes, and arrives again the moment of the Yurupari ritual. We do the incantations to arrange the world and prepare the ritual again.

Each new important step for the apprentice is done during a Yurupari ritual. Remember that it was during this ceremony that he was placed shamanic elements in his body by means of an incantation. *Every year, a ritual to reorder (or re-arrange) the world must first be done before any Yurupari ritual.*

Then, during a new Yurupari ritual, the apprentice is observed by a shaman to verify that his shamanic elements have developed normally.

It is assumed that the shaman is endowed with clairvoyance (Principle 8), since it is this that would allow him to see the state of the shamanic elements invisible in the body of the apprentice. *He would even sometimes have a clairaudiance* (Principle 9) since he could also hear the words of Yurupari.

If the apprentice has deteriorated his shamanic elements, it implies that he has not respected the diet (because of Principle 6). It must then be removed because of the following principle: *An apprentice may die if the shamanic elements placed in his body are too deteriorated* (Principle 10)

To remove them, the shaman then pronounces a special incantation. And as for the one that closes a Yurupari ritual for other young men, he invokes all the foods so that they can be consumed again.

When the apprentice has managed to endure several years of diet and has thus been able to sustainably strengthen his shamanic powers, the shaman can also reduce his restrictions by an incantation of salt that allow him to consume a little bit of it, or to tolerate heat sources. But that does not last.

The first yagé intake

> It is then that we do the incantations of the *yagé* (ayahuasca), so that the apprentice can drink some. He receives a little bit, and gradually so that he can begin to see the world by his thought. Then, he is still put on a very strict diet. He then spends his time vomiting until the end of the ritual. Once the Yurupari is gone again, the novices' food is still being

processed, while the apprentice shaman will have to continue his diet and stay in the forest. In the morning, he must go to the forest to vomit all day long. Above all, he can't swallow any fruit. Not even touch the tree or the leaf. He must walk slowly and carefully to avoid exposure to danger. He comes back only at nightfall, to collapse in his hammock without saying a word. An old woman is then specially designated to prepare his food. She gives him a thin piece of cassava bread of pure manioc starch, and some manioc beer. Once he has eaten, he rests for a while. Then he gets up to sit next to the elders and listen to the shamanic words. When we do the incantations of his learning, we prepare him for that. The elders say to him: "If you see the adults chewing coca, you must go chew with them." They will not insist saying: "Get out of here, come here." They only tell him once. Then he sits with them until midnight. Afterwards, he goes to rest for a moment, and gets up around half past two in the morning. He takes a bath and vomit. He comes out of the water about three o'clock in the morning. Then he comes back and sits outside the roundhouse. He can't enter. In the twilight, he returns to the forest. And he begins vomiting again. This is his work during a year. Then we arrange the world again for another Yurupari ritual. And the young men still take the initiation until the end of the ritual. We check his body again to see if he has followed the diet and obeyed the recommendations. We still give the incantations of the *yagé* to make him drink and see the world by his thought. After the Yurupari ritual, we still treat the food of teenagers and men who initiated them. Only the shaman apprentice must continue his diet. Many are afraid of being subjected to such a diet, but they don't have to be discouraged. They must know how to strengthen their spirit. And a new year of diet passes.

The yagé or ayahuasca is a liana of the genus *Banisteriopsis* (called *kaphi* in yucuna) used to prepare a hallucinogenic beverage. Yucuna-speaking Indians do not usually consume it. Mario and other healers pointed out to me that it was not necessary, since they could acquire their powers and memorize their incantations without consuming it. Other healers have called on neighboring Tucano-speaking ethnic groups who traditionally consume one of the most powerful varieties of yagé and reserve them for the initiation rituals. Milciades Yucuna, Pedro and Fermín Rodriguez have taken yagé with the Macuna, and another Matapi shaman from Quebrada Negra (low Mirití-Paraná river) has also taken it with the Cubeo. According to many healers, the yagé has the effect of giving visions that allow to see the spirits who teach the incantations, but the diet becomes all the more severe and dangerous. Since he has taken yagé, the young man must continue after the Yurupari ritual not only the diet, but also most of his trials.

Questioning

Still comes the moment of arranging the world to perform a Yurupari ritual. During the rite, the apprentice has to pass new tests again. We still check his body to see how he followed the diet. He can't swallow anything. We really keep our eyes on him. Just in case he would sneakily swallow a berry. As he is about to finish his training, he is even more fragile. At least fruit which he could swallow, it's over for him. So we have to really take care of him to avoid this until the end of the ritual. After that, we treat the food again, while the apprentice is still on the diet. Then I say to him: "Now you will stay two months with me." We say that to see if he really respected the diet. He always returns in a similar way to the roundhouse. Then at midnight, he must go to the water. We say to Kajyuwaka, the eldest Yurupari, to get up and accompany him to go to bathe. In case he doesn't go to the water to vomit... Kajyuwaka orders him to go to vomit. He wakes him only once to force him to get up. If he does not get up, Kajyuwaka kicks him out from his hammock, and gives him a big whip in the back. That removes at once all his laziness. Then his body is coated with pepper juice. And so (after spending the day in forest) at each nightfall, he returns to the roundhouse, and directly collapses in his hammock.

The old woman always gives him a piece of cassava bread of pure manioc starch. The part with which he holds the piece between his fingers must be discarded.

If he wants to eat everything, he must grab the piece with a leaf. After eating, he will rest for a moment until he is asked to come. He is then given a seat to sit down. He is asked: – Now little boy, tell what you did in the forest. What did you see? Fruits maybe? You haven't eaten them at least? Here you can't hide anything. Better to reveal everything immediately, because anyway, we will test you to find out it. We see very well in his body the traces of the bad things he did. So he is questioned to see if he really respected his diet. He says: "I didn't do anything wrong. It went well." If he hides the fact of having eaten a fruit,[13] we can see it. So we ask him again. And if he still denies the truth, we get angry. – So it's like that, you didn't do anything! But a bit later I'm going to look at your body. Then I will know where you have gone, and I will not tell you anything. Then he is scared. He thinks: "Why didn't I tell him everything?" The shaman tells to someone: "Go get me three canes to whip him." This one picks them up and brings to him. Then the shaman holds a calabash to him saying: "Crush the pepper in this calabash, it must become very thick and red." Then he pronounces the incantations to remove the impure food he has absorbed. In the meantime, the young man remains seated and wonders what awaits him. When the shaman finishes treating the pepper and the canes, he says to the apprentice: "I'm going to look at you outside, to see if you tell the truth." He looks at him outside, and says to him: "Here you can hide nothing from me!" He then takes a cigar to observe him, and breathes on his body. Then he visualizes how his walk was in the forest to see what he did. He then sees if the apprentice has eaten sylvan fruits. If he detects *Jessenia* fruit in his body, he blows tobacco smoke on it to remove that, and the fruit falls in his hand. "And that, what is it? You said that you hadn't swallowed anything! I told you not to eat the fruits you could find in the forest! But you hid it from me,

---

[13] Fermín told me one day that he had made this mistake precisely, even though he was in the same phase of learning, and he regretted it. Here he relates his own experience.

whereas I told you that you have to endure the diet to acquire the shamanic power that you wanted. Maybe with that, you won't want to do this again! Then he takes the three canes and makes him whipped. Many men start whipping his back. Then they take the pepper. "That's what you deserve!" And the shaman sends him to vomit to throw out the fruits he has swallowed. Some come out overwhelmed, sad or discouraged, but one must keep the spirit strong, it is in one's own interest to listen to the advices. It's not because they want them badly that they beat them. If they do not flog them, the disease lies in wait for them. Then the apprentice is left alone during two months. Until Kajyuwaka does not have any more anger after him. Therefore, this apprentice who has been told so many incantat-ions, so much history, retains almost nothing. He has lost all his spirits. Some of them have enough, and say to themselves: "How is it possible that I know nothing? They lied to me or what? It's been so long since I am enduring the diet." Then some people want their food processed to end the diet. And when they do this treatment, they will remain without anything, as if they had never learned anything. But if the apprentice doesn't get tired, and assumes an even stronger diet, his jaguar mantle can develop again. And the power of incantations increases accordingly. The Jaguar Ancestor esteems him even more. When he has endured such a diet, they begin to treat him so that he can eat more varied foods. Then he can start talking with his mother and his brothers. From there, he doesn't need to vomit so regularly. Other shamans want to kill him, to remove his jaguar mantle, and his power to memorize incantations. If they strip him like this, the apprentice is left with nothing. This is why you must always pay attention to the diet. A jaguar-man could always kill him while he is no longer under the protection of the Jaguar Ancestor. And he is tested again to see if he really follows the advice. A new year still passes. We arrange the world again to prepare a new Yurupari ritual. By the incantation, we estimate how long the rite of initiation will have to last. The apprentice suffers a lot in this test. We still pronounce for him the incantations of *yagé* so that he could drink it again. Then the shaman says to him: "I'm going to look at you one last time to see if you really listened to the recommendations." Then we look at him in detail. If we see that he has listened well to the recommendations, or that he endured more diet than what was asked of him, we are very satisfied. The shaman says to him: "You listened well to the advice, because you wanted to receive the power of the elders. So I'm going to start giving you this power." While the others pass the Yurupari ritual, we make him swallow the *yagé*. We tell him in detail all the myth of the Yurupari. Sat next to an elder, he must repeat everything from the beginning to the end. Then he must recite entirely *the Incantation of Preparation of the Yurupari Ritual, the Incantation of Preparation of the Teenagers*, and *the Incantation of the End-of-Diet of the Teenagers*. He must not forget anything.

Fermín is well aware of the lack of diet of which he speaks, because he himself lived it and bitterly regretted like many other apprentices healers. This subjective experience is much more important for acquiring such certitudes than simply listening to the teachings of healers, or observing the results of their cures. His certainties are mainly based on his experience of the amplification of his psychic and sensory abilities, and it is this experience that has given him the courage to persevere in such a long asceticism. Fermín noticed a marked improvement in his memory when he respected the diet. And he frequently experienced altered states of consciousness caused by prolonged fasts, sleep restrictions, and yagé catches. Such astral journeys have aroused in him visions in which mythical spirits and ancestors have appeared.

During the Yurupari trials, he saw and heard Kajyuwaka follow and guide him. Kajyuwaka is the elder brother of Yurupari Ancestor, born from the calcined remains of the latter. All those who pass the ritual dread Kajyuwaka because he is perceived as severe, irascible and ruthless.

Fermín also experienced forgetting all the incantations he had learned after only eating a forbidden fruit. Fortunately for him, this slight infraction could be made up by new tests of purification, that is to say by *vomiting*, *floggings*, and *absorption of pepper juice* by the nostrils. The shamanic objects placed in his body were thus cleaned and recovered. But Fermín also had to be *isolated* for *repenting*, and it is on this condition, which pre-supposes absolute certainty in his convictions, that he was able to redouble his efforts in asceticism and definitively renounce any failure on the diet. Later, when he became a shaman instructor, he had the same visions as his master to perceive prohibited foods by blowing tobacco on the body of the apprentice. It is clear, then, that when one begins to engage in shamanism, the experience of the learner itself leaves no room for doubt about the importance of the pursuit of trials in the development of their powers.

Flagellation during a Yurupari ritual.

Knowledge of the world

He is given some *yagé* so that he may well perceive in his visions[14] all that has been said to him. That is why we must respect the diet: to memorize quickly all the words we are taught. Then he must fully explain how we remove diseases and how we meet the Yurupari. And it must list all the diseases of this earth. Always without forgetting anything. Then we must tell how we see the world and how it was created. From the point of view of our shamanic thought, it is small this world where we live. Since it was created, the Scolopendra Ancestor (centipede) is rolled up around it. It has the spirit of anaconda, and as it is rolled up on itself, the world is seated on it. That's why all the thoughts of the people come together in him. As for the demons, they watch over the Scolopendra Ancestor. If a bad person tries to make fun of him, the world can be destroyed. If the apprentice wants, he can verify that the Scolopendra Ancestor is able to shake the Earth. He just has to tell to the Demon Ancestor[15]:

– Grandpa, I have a request for you. I would like to test this Scolopendra Ancestor by touching him with the tip of my club. Here are the offerings that I brought to you: coca, snuff, a cigar. If the Demon Ancestor agrees, he says:

– Well my grandson, to touch him, I must also hold the club with my hand.

– Okay, grandpa. So one takes his club and the Demon Ancestor seizes it too. "You will have the proof immediately." No sooner had we touched the Scolopendra Ancestor than he moved his whole body. And the earth begins to quake. The Demon Ancestor then says:

– That's enough, my grandson. It's scary to think of what could happen. It's so huge!

---

[14] **Yuwera'kajo** (Yuc.). Get drunk. To be in a second state.

[15] **Jiñá Chi'narikana** (Yuc.). *Abuelo de los Demonios, Diablo* (Span.). Ancestor of the Demons, also called "Devil".

And the apprentice has to explain it all. He has to say: "So was created the world on this earth..." He must list and describe the ills controlled by the tapirs. Likewise with their snakes-arrows, and the dizzy spells they may engender. Same thing with the ills of the brocket deers. Their snakes produce dizzy spells and diseases. Their traps give vomiting. Then he has to tell about the telluric spirits *jarechina*, their ills, and how they appeared. Then, the jaguars' ills, and how they appeared. For each one of them, he must know how they appeared in this world and enumerate the diseases they control.

He has to list all the masters of this world: the giant monkeys *kuwañá*, the monsters *chu'wí*, the ogresses *kuwayuká*[16], with the dizzy spells they engender. He must explain how the season of the big *mawa* frogs unfolds, and what their ills are. He has to tell also about the season of the *pumarú* frogs' ills. Then it comes the season of the upstream migration of fish. He must list their diseases, the attacks they inflict and their snakes. After that, it comes the season of the caterpillars' ills: their many illnesses and forms of fainting. He has to explain how to heal their infections. Then, he must tell how Kamarari (the God of Thunder) has appeared. Then, he has to tell about the appearance of the female devils called *Naayona*, how they burn the souls of people. The appearance of the Lake Kerawiyú, and the origin of the Demon Ancestor. One must describe how one sees the world by going around it by one's thought. The apprentice is told:

– We see many things, and also women *nachana* (animal spirits)[17]. Above all, if you see such women, do not talk to them. If they talk to you, you go straight without answering. If you talk to them, they kill you. In addition, the Yurupari is always ready to kill you until you have not finished your training.

---

[16] **Kuwayuká** (Yuc.). *Madremonte* (Span.). Supernatural woman having only one breast (such as an Amazon). They are supposed to eat termites. Very feared, they would have the power to change some hunters lost in shaman. It is said that when a person is so transformed, the spirit of it seems to have disappeared, as if replaced by a new mysterious spirit.

[17] **Inaana nachana** (Yuc.). These women would be apparitions of animal spirits.

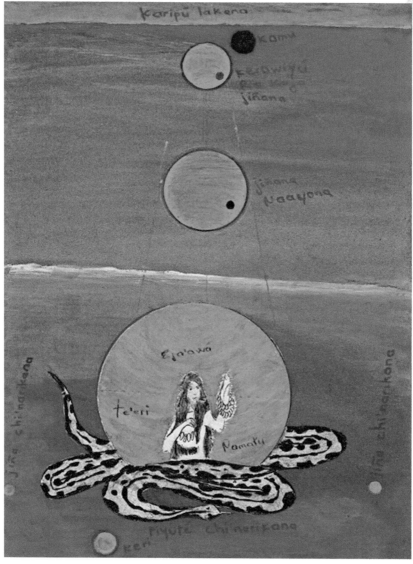

Karipú Lakena: Four Grandchildren of Karipú.
Kamu: Sun. *Kerawiyú:* Lake Kerawiyú. *Re kaja jiñana:* There are also demons.
Jiñana Naayona: The female devils Naayona.
Eja'wá: World. *Te'eri:* Earth. *Ñamatu:* Mother of the Earth. *Keri:* Moon.
Piyuté chi'narikana: Scolopendra-Anaconda ancestor.
Jiña chi'narikana: Demon Ancestor.

If you disobey, we won't be able to do anything for you. We explain and enumerate the different paths of jaguars, which are actually light rays, like lightning. They can also walk through tornadoes and the whirlpools, both by the wind and by the water. As the traces left by water bugs (*Gerris*) that can walk on the surface of water, the jaguars can also take them to cross the rivers. They also have underground paths. This goes back to the day when the Earthworm Ancestor killed Jiyánama's mother, and managed to escape from him by fleeing under the earth. Since then, the jaguars has also begun to control (in part) these underground passages.

Once the apprentice has reached an advanced stage of learning, larger yagé intakes make him see the world in ever greater detail in order to know it perfectly. When he is able to invoke all the important elements of this world and arrange it in incantations, he can move on to the next step which is this time to act on the world. By means of the usual offerings (coca, snuff, cigar), he can shake the earth by asking the Demon Ancestor to hold his club with him to touch the centipede that surrounds the world. The young man realizes how his privileged encounters with powerful ancestors give him a devastating power.

It is the same with all the ancestors of animals and other masters of the forest. The apprentice must be able to invoke their names, their origins, their sacred places and their evils, in order to be able to control them by means of certain magic words. It is only on this condition that he can then borrow from each of them their envelopes and their weapons. But such encounters are never safe.

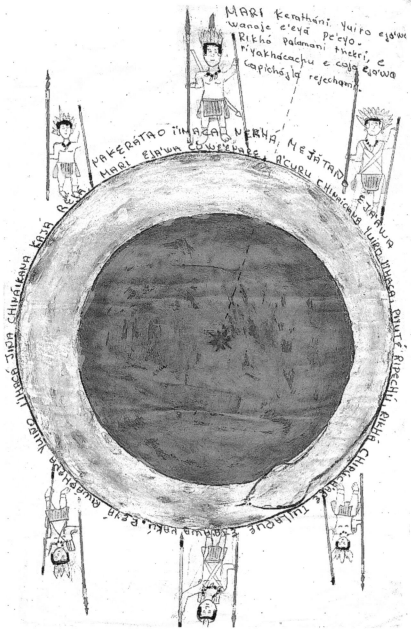

Scolopendra-Anaconda Ancestor surrounding the World.

Learning with the Jaguars and the Karipú's Grandsons

Visit of the apprentice alone

It is then necessary to explain how the thought can go to find the jaguar ancestors and the Karipú's Grandsons. The shaman says to the apprentice:

– When I will send you to their home, you will jump from one stone to another. Regularly, you must develop your muscles by hammering them with a stick in the river to be strong enough[18]. Because the jaguar mantle that you will wear then is very heavy. One goes up with that. When you look at this stone, you think that it is near and that you will jump on it quickly. But in fact, it is distant. Then, you have what you deserve. If you haven't bathed enough, and haven't vomited enough, you can then fall into the precipice, and it's over. But if you have vomited sufficiently, you arrive directly on it, because you are strong enough. Then, you continue to reach another stone. There, is seated a large jaguar tied with a chain. No sooner had he seen someone approaching than he wants to kill him. In the middle of the road, he is guarding the passage. But one must not be afraid of him.

It is only if we ate forbidden things that we have to be afraid of him. Then one thinks: "He may kill me." And one can't pass. For lack of the necessary knowledge, one can only turn back. But if one has respected the diet, there is nothing to fear. It can be held by the neck. It remains quiet, and licks one's whole body. So one can pass.

Then one reaches the Karipú's Grandsons and the Jaguar Ancestor. The apprentice is told: "Here are the Karipú's Grandsons." But only a huge rock can be seen. "Here, the cigar must be used." And one blows tobacco smoke on the rock. It is then transformed into roundhouse. We enter it. This is where the Karipú's Grandsons and the Jaguar Ancestor put him to the test one last time, before giving him the last recommendations. As always, one must not answer.

---

[18] To become strong, teens are expected to bathe as frequently as possible in the river and hammer daily all the muscles of the body with a stick.

If they offer you coca, you do not even have to chew it, just pretend. If they blow you tobacco smoke by the nostrils, you will already have a shamanic bamboo tube[19] (put by incantation) that enters through the nostrils and goes out through the mouth. Thus, this tobacco will go out directly, and they can't do anything. Because this coca and tobacco belong to the gods. It is not for us. If one tries to chew such a coca, or to inhale such a tobacco, one would be quickly affected by nausea and by madness. And one ends up dying of it. Then they test the apprentice to see if he is really able to respect the diet.

All the forbidden foods appear to him: fresh meat of white-lipped peccary, smoked weevil larvae, etc. And all the forbidden wild fruits: sylvan abiu, abiu of the woodland, avocado, etc. One must then be very careful. He is warned: "If you see such things appear, do not pay attention, do not even look at them! Otherwise, if you do not listen, and eat them, your spirit will immediately be swallowed by the Yurupari. And your spirit will be destroyed forever.

If you obey and do not give in to this temptation, they will give you other recommendations, exactly as I speak right now." Then, the ancestors tell him all the shamanic words, especially those that can remove the diseases. They say everything very quickly, in barely five minutes. That is when he has to do a U-turn. And the Yurupari also returns. Once the latter is gone, we can do again the treatment of end of diet. But the apprentice must still follow his diet.

Arrived at an advanced stage of his shamanic mastery, the apprentice must go alone to visit the Jaguar Ancestor and the Karipú's Grandsons. The diet is still essential to pass in front of such important ancestors because at several times, they control or put him to the test of the diet, always ready to kill him at the slightest fault.

---

[19] **Kewiri** (Yuc.). Bamboo tube for making pan flutes (*chirulo* in Spanish). This tube was previously placed there by pronouncing certain incantatory words.

But the young man must *also have developed enough his muscles by hammering them daily with a stick in a river.* Although it is less and less common today, many elders admit to having practiced this technique of bodybuilding in their youth. Considered very effective, it would have forged many generations of warriors since time immemorial.

The apprentice must also *have received an incantation to place a tube in the nasal cavity.* This protection would allow him to reject entirely the coca powder offered by the Ancestors.

Finally, he must *be able to use tobacco and the incantations* he has been taught to transform the rock of the Karipú's Grandsons into Maloca.

Surrender of powers

He is said: "You only have one year left to complete the incantations of your preparation. Then I will give you the load of the elders' power. You will then be free to live as you want, and to eat what you want. I will not have to interfere anymore. Nevertheless, you'll be grateful all my life, for what I did for you to acquire this power.

And the apprentice endures one more year of diet. Then, the incantations which regulate the world and prepare the Yurupari ritual are done again, in order to finish the formation of the apprentice. Then all the shamans and healers are ceremonially invited, to declare that the apprentice has completed his training. If it is true, he is allowed to assume this load. And they must respect him as a shaman. If we do not inform them, they may not respect him as such. Without an official declaration, they do not have to know it. That is why we must inform all the elders.

It is then that the yagé is given again to the apprentice to make him see the world as a whole. This time, he has to drink a lot of that. He is often given so that, in his second state of consciousness, he could see very well the world. It is then that we need a godfather to watch him, because he could run away, or have too strong hallucinations.

MAIKE PECHUJUMI JACHU'KO
CHI'INAIKA LOKO'PANI

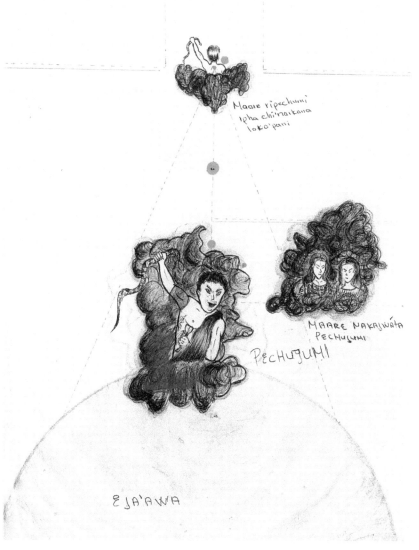

The spirit of apprentice who has passed all the trials goes directly to meet the Ancestors while others have to discipline their minds.

Then his godfather remains on guard with him. It is during this ritual that the young apprentice offers to the shaman instructor all kinds of offerings: coca, snuff, snail shell snuff box, seat, calabash holder, calabash, cigar, necklace of jaguar canines, club, jingle bells, maracas. And even basketries: cassava colander, cassava sieve, manioc dough boa spinner, and basket. The shaman instructor thus receives all the necessary goods to complete the formation of the apprentice. They are those goods which make possible to go to seek the shamanic powers that the apprentice had requested the Jaguar Ancestor. The spirit of all these offerings must be brought to the ancestors. So we go back to see them. Coming to the Karipú's Grandsons and Ancestor Jaguar, we offer them the spirit of coca, tobacco, snuffbox, siege, jaguar canines, etc. Everything must be brought to them. One says to them: "These are the offerings that are for you." And we offer these to them. Then one says:

– I came to seek the shamanic things that I had requested you. That's the reason for my coming, grandfather.

– Well, grandson. Since you came for that, we will give them to re is the power of the ancestors, you can take it. Bring our grandson, the one you have trained, to see how he will assume this power.

– Well, grandfather. So one takes these shamanic things and brings them back to this earth. That is when we inform the shamans and healers: "Now, I will give this apprentice the ancestors' power, in exchange for the offerings that have been made. Then the apprentice is taken outside. The Yurupari starts to turn around him. Then he is seated in the middle of his seat. To make him receive all the power of the jaguars, he is told: "Here is the ancestors' power that you have wanted, for which you had to assume the diet, and which will make you earn the ancestors' words. These words will enable you to become a man. That is why one must assume the diet. In the past, we almost never let anybody have this power. In order to prevent others from misusing it.

And if you behave badly with the new generations, this same power can cause your loss. Only if you make good use of this power, you can hope to live long with it. It is then that we place in him the jaguar mantle, the jaguar mirror, the gloves to remove diseases, the power to throw lightning, the auditory little balls to get one's bearings in order to move as a jaguar. With all this, the apprentice's spirit is heavy. And as he is already in another state with the yagé, some things appear to him. He sees a traditional seat like a boa rolled up on itself, trees like people; everything is transformed in his eyes. The other shamans appear to him like jaguars, and he can see their spirit directly thanks to the power given to him.

Then he is told: – Now my boy, you will see with your own eyes the things I told you. You must know them already. If you do not know them, I can't help you. The shaman and his apprentice then speak together to make a last clarification. Then the shaman takes the apprentice's spirit to the jaguar ancestors. The climb is done by singing in the language of jaguars. We jump up to a stone. Then, singing again in that same language, we leap to another stone. We then arrive at the place where the jaguar is sitting. One says to the young man who was trained: "Now, it's up to you to go ahead. Above all, don't be afraid. I already told you how to go." Then the young man moves forward, and the jaguar prepares to jump on him. But the apprentice seizes him by the neck. Then the jaguar softens, and licks him all over the body to purify him of the last forbidden foods which could stay there. Then we go to see the Karipú's Grandsons. One says to the apprentice: "There live the Karipú's Grandsons. Those who are told so many adventures. You are going to see them with your own eyes. The apprentice sees nothing but a huge rock. So one tells to him: "I am going to explain to you how a cigar is used. We blow tobacco smoke on this rock and it will turn into roundhouse. And we make him listen to the necessary incantation. There, once the incantation has been pronounced, we say to him: "Now you will see how I blow tobacco smoke on this rock."

Then we blow at several different places of the rock, then it starts to make noise. We hear people inside. And the rock appears in the form of a large roundhouse. But it then resumes its rock form. One then says to the apprentice: "It's your turn now. I want to see if you really learned the words of your ancestors. If you know them, you should succeed. Otherwise, we just have to go back. One gives the cigar to him. And he must pronounce the incantation[20]. He blows tobacco smoke at the different places of the rock. Then it starts to make noise, and turns into roundhouse. One then enters with the apprentice. The Jaguar and the Karipú's Grandsons Ancestor are there. One says to them:

– I brought the young man that I formed, to introduce him to you.

– Well, grandson, they reply. So he is the one who wants to receive the ancestors' power. And they show him a seat. That is when the spirits of different things appear to him. All forbidden foods. But the apprentice doesn't pay attention. They are testing him.

And they still make recommendations to him in a severe tone. They say to him: "Grandson, you want to receive the ancestors' power. But it is very dangerous. Jaguar shamans can use it to destroy you. But since you want to receive it, I advise you not use it to harm others. Make good use of it: be compassionate towards the new generations by healing and removing their ills. From here we can see how you use it. You can't hide from us. Because we created everything that exists on Earth, everything belongs to us. And the Ancestor Jaguar makes him listen to all the incantations, like the one which can extract the diseases. No word is missing. Then he shows him the Earth. "Here is the Earth. It is tiny. So was it created. The Scolopendra Ancestor is rolled up around it. These demons have custody of him. Here also meet some ancestors of humans. From here, we can turn around the Earth. This is also from here the masters of this world send diseases there.

---

[20] As this one contains only other incantation parts that he has already learned, he must above all remember the structure of this new incantation that he has just listened.

Then he explains who are the female devils called *Naayona* responsible for burning the deads' souls. Then he tells the story of the God of Thunder. And the history of Lake Kerawiyú. How was it created, and what is it for? Then they say to the apprentice: "These are the demons who guard the Lake Kerawiyú. The Ja'timaja (elder tribe of Tanimuca Indians) have left them there and they are still there. They are the ghosts of their ancestors." With his eyes, the young man sees them in real. Then, one takes back the apprentice's spirit on this earth, where we are practicing the Yurupari. Then one says to him: "Now you go extract something for me to see if you really know the shamanic words of your ancestors. So the apprentice removes from his shaman instructor who taught his jaguar mantle. And he pulls out all the other magical things. Then one says to him: "That's good, my boy, you've followed the advices. Now it is my turn to extract the jaguar's magical things from you. The shaman extracts the mantle, and all the other things of the jaguar. Then he gives them back to him in his body. From this point on, one can leave him such a power. We inform then the shamans and the healers so that they know that they must respect him as such. After that, we let go the Yurupari. We treat the food to finish the diet of the adolescents. Then we treat especially that of the apprentice who has achieved his training. We treat all the foods for him. Finally he is said: "From now on you can eat all the foods, because that is why they were created. During the learning, one must respect the diet. It is not without pain that things come in our mind. From now on, you can live as you want, I do not have to watch you anymore. However you will owe me your gratitude during the rest of my life. Now you will rest for a year. Then you will be able to start healing. Then, one is left alone. It is through suffering that one learns the words of the ancestors. One feels loneliness. One then goes alone in forest. After one year, one starts to cure, and will continue until the end of one's days.

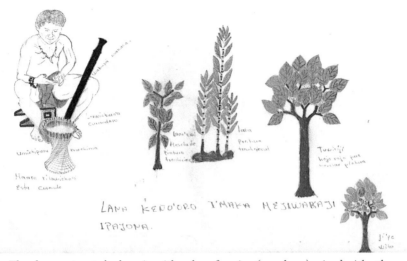

The shaman treats body pain with a dye of genipa (yuc. lana) mixed with other plants (lane'ewi, tuwirijí, ji'ye).

During the last year of training, the apprentice must first know how to recite all the necessary incantations, including the longest ones like the *Incantation to reorder the world*, to receive the requested powers. He must then prepare enough offerings for the shaman instructor and the shaman ancestors. Then, during one of the last Yurupari rituals, he must take the yagé to visit in spiritual form the shaman ancestors and respect all the recommendations necessary for their meeting. There, he has to prove himself by exposing everything he has learned. Finally, on his return to real life, he must be able to use his shamanic skills in front of his master.

The latter then leaves to the young man the extraordinary attributes of jaguar shamans that can be borrowed at will: a feline body mantle to move with agility, a mirror to see at night or at a distance, jaguar gloves to extract the diseases, a thundering club symbolizing the arm of a jaguar, and auditory balls giving it an exceptional listening acuity.

After handing over these powers, the shaman master informs the other healers that the youth has completed his training. He then closes the Yurupari ritual and treats the apprentice's food to end his diet.

Acquire the attributes of spirit-masters

The coats of *chu'wí* monsters

The forest masters' powers are acquired in the same way. If one wants to acquire a mantle of the *chu'wí* monsters, one can go to request it from them. The same offerings must be brought to them: coca, snuff, cigar. These monsters also live like humans in their roundhouse. Arriving there, one says to them: "I came to get one of your mantles to use it in my travels, grandfather. Here are the offerings I brought for you. That is when they offer him coca, snuff, cigar, calabash holder, calabash. Then they say: "Well, grandson. As you have offered me this, we will lend you one for a moment only. Such mantle could easily kill you. It happens when you don't have the control of it. Then they ask: "Which one will you take, my grandson?

Look, and choose the one you like. So we choose. Many bodies (mantles) are hanging[21]. They are hung like bark fiber shirts! They are very beautiful. A bright nut[22] is hung in each of them, with on the inside the power to inflict faintings, and other weakenings. One says to them:

– Lend me this one, grandfathers.

– Well, grandson. So they take it down and make him put it on. They tell him:

– There you have it! We lend it to you just a moment. After, you have to return it. So one takes it, and brings it back. With that, one can go far in the forest, where there is no one anymore. One puts this body of *chu'wí*, and so one takes this form. In the nut, there is some red chica pigment (*Arrabidaea chica*) whose spirit comes to paint our face. It weakens people, makes them feel dizzy, because of the forbidden foods they could have eaten. If you want to test this to see if it's true, you cry out and immediately scratch the chica paint that you have on the face. Then you make a gesture in the direction of the person you are aiming for, and the spirit of the chica rushes on it.

---

[21] Here the author uses the term *ritami*, which means "body", instead of *a'rumaka* ("clothing"). These "clothes" actually appear as bodies.

[22] **Tuphí** (Yuc.). Coco of palm *Astrocaryum sp.*

Then, he faints and can lose his memory. A little later, a particular sound crosses the forest. The *chu'wí* also have other corporeal envelopes such as those of the tayra[23], the short-eared dog[24] or the giant anteater to scare children who have eaten prohibited foods. In those envelopes, you can move as you want. When you have enough, you remove this envelope of *chu'wí* to recover human form. Then you give them back. You tell them:

– I bring your things back to you.

– Well, my grandson. You can come and borrow them whenever you want.

– Thank you. Then some pepper must be shamanically treated. And one has to absorb it by the nostrils to reject anything that could give you nausea, in case of some of one's soul would have remained in the mantle of *chu'wí*. That way, there is no risk. Otherwise, part of one's soul could stay with the *chu'wí* monsters. One weakens oneself and one can end up dying. And the rest of one's soul goes back to their home. We don't joke with that.

Human shamans can not permanently acquire the attributes of animals or masters of the forest. But they have the opportunity to borrow their body envelopes and weapons, if they go to find the masters to make them the request with the usual offerings. As with anything borrowed from humans, the shaman has to respect the instructions for use of the masters, and give them back early enough.

The *chu'wí* monsters are masters of the plant *Arrabidaea chica* whose red pigment is used in witchcraft among the Yucuna and other neighboring populations of Tucano language (Macuna, Desana, Barasana). This pigment would have the power to weaken the person's mind and limit its possibilities of action. Each coat of *chu'wí* is endowed with a chica-filled nut to take control of a prey paralyzing it with fright. This pigment explains why the tayra, the

---

[23] **Yu'wé** (Yuc.). *Zorro* (Vernacular Spanish). *Eira barbara.*
[24] **Juwálake** (Yuc.). *Perro de monte* (Ver. Span.). *Atelocynus microtis.*

short-eared dog and the giant anteater frighten children who have eaten forbidden foods. But the use of such envelopes and weapons is obviously never safe for the human borrower, even after returning them. A shamanic purification with pepper juice is sometimes necessary.

The weapons of the giant apes

There are also the giant apes *kuwañá*. In their world[25], they also live like humans in their roundhouse. If one wants to visit them, one must also prepare them coca, snuff and cigar. Then one goes to meet them by spiritual path. Once arrived in front of them, one says to them: "I came to borrow your weapons, grandfathers. One offers the coca brought for them. And one says to them:
– I would like to ask you to lend me this type of weapon.
– Well, my grandson. Choose the one you want. And there are many hung. Some have harpy eagle feathers, they have a jaguar spirit. "Lend me that one." Then they take it down and hold it out, saying: "We just lend it to you for a moment, you have to give it back to us because it could kill you. So, one receives it and takes it very far in the forest, where there is no one. When we use this weapon of jaguar, we transform ourselves into this animal. The soul changes as well, and we are no longer really human. Once in this body, we walk in the forest to kill prey. As for the *kajilá*[26] we received, its spirit ends up in our jaguar teeth. And that is what we plant in the game. When we look at its tracks left on the prey, we say that the jaguar bit him. But in his spirit, he pierced him with his spear. That's why he doesn't miss his target. He kills it on his first try. When we are tired of walking in such a jaguar body, we remove it and we return it to the giant apes *kuwañá*. One says to them:
– I give you your weapon back.
– Well, my grandson. Come and borrow it whenever you like.
Then one returns. Also, one must treat pepper and snuff to be

---

[25] **Apú chuwá** (Yuc.). Literally: "By their path (spiritual)". One can also translate by "in their parallel or spiritual universe".

[26] **Kajilá** (Yuc.). Short spear about the size of an arrow.

sure to recover one's whole soul, in case of some of one's soul would have remained in the weapon. This avoids any danger. This thing isn't a harmless game. And if you want to move in the body of the *Kuwayuká* women (forest masters), you can also ask them. In the same way, you can request the same thing from the Utula'yu spirits, the machaka dwarves, the boas, the water masters *pá'yumi*, the rays. You can even borrow the clothes of fish. These were created for them in the same way.

Always in their waking dreams, shamans can acquire from the giant apes *kuwañá* weapons that transform them into jaguars. What is the result of this transformation? The ancients say that once shamans were able to physically transform into a jaguar, but today such transformations are only the privilege of the last few great shamans of remote tribes. According to Fermín, it would nevertheless be possible to get into trance to momentarily project one's mind into the body of a jaguar and take control of it at distance. This animal reincorporation of the spirit would necessarily influence his free will by giving him an irresistible obsession for hunting, and a redoubtable efficiency which cannot fail his target. This impact of the body on the mind is one of the implications of the perspectivism that is found everywhere in Native America (De Castro, 1996) and in animist societies (Descola, 2013), according to which the point of view of a species always depends on the body where it resides. Thus the remote controlled jaguar can kill animals or humans (perceived at these times as game) for the shaman. Ordinary people do not directly perceive any remote animal embodying and may ignore them. Nevertheless, the spiritual change of the shaman remains still detectable because of his new behaviors. Everyone can see the frequent isolation of the shaman to go into a trance, and his insatiable obsession for the bloody quest for new prey (*History of Ka'mari, History of Karupe*). That's why when the shaman left his jaguar mantle to come back among the humans, a treatment with snuff and pepper juice (to absorb by the nostrils) is necessary to recover his whole mind and become enough "human" again to no longer see his congeners as prey.

The incense of resurrection of the popes vultures

As for the king vultures ancestors, they also received many things. Their greatest shamanism power is that of *pójori*, an incense which can bring deads to life. When someone dies, we can go ask them. Then we make him feel, and he regains consciousness. But they hardly accept to lend it. It is very expensive. In exchange, they can ask for a son, a parent, a brother. But it is very bad to sacrifice a close family member in exchange. If we don't do it, they say: "You have to pay with your life!" So it's better not to take such an incense. However some bad shamans take it, and pay it with the life of a parent or a brother. We can't pay with the life of someone else. If someone takes such an incense, the Yurupari thinks it's very bad. Then he curses him. He says to him: "It is not to do this kind of thing that I left you the power of the ancestors. After such a mistake, you must die." And the person doesn't live very long. That's why we must not ask for the incense of the king vultures. It's far too expensive to pay with the life of a person.

According to the Yucuna, king vultures would have the power to resurrect the dead. Mario had told me that he could not get rid of the king vultures who killed his chickens around his maloca. He had noticed that every time he shot one of them with a rifle, not only did the body of the scavenger mysteriously disappear the next day, but he found another identical one nearby a few times later.

Milciades and Fermín respect the king vultures because they have the reputation of being masters in shamanic warfare (*Myth of Yewákumi*, who had taken a king vulture wife) and especially because they would know evil incantations extremely secret that shamans should not normally know unless they want to be able to kill humans: this is *the Incantation of Protection after a Murder*, and *The Incantation to Resurrect the Dead*.

When the Yucuna shamans are accused of having killed someone by witchcraft, they generally defend themselves by saying that it is impossible for them to perform such an act on pain of the fatal sanction of shaman ancestors (Karipú's Grandsons, Yurupari, Jaguar Ancestor), even those who lent them their powers. But I also heard Milciades told a relative that at a drinking evening where he was challenged on incantatory knowing, he ended up showing his superiority by uttering extracts from the incarnation of the king vultures and ending by *the Incantation of Protection after a Murder* (Fontaine, 2015; 2017). The fact that Milciades sometimes boasts about knowing this incantation explains why he is as much feared and respected as accused of witchcraft killings. Such an incantation would give him the opportunity not to be immediately sanctioned by the ancestors.

As for *The Incantation to Resurrect the Dead*, it refers to the *Myth of the King Vulture* (Mario Matapi, 2006) in which the later offers a remedy to wake up the dead. But Fermín indicates here that it is necessary to sacrifice in return the life of a close relative. So better not to use it, especially if you risk to be cursed by the Yurupari. But I have already heard such accusations from shamans who would have appealed to king vultures, having suddenly lost their wife or father-in-law, to save their son whom everyone thought he was doomed.

The weapons of tapirs

Likewise with the tapirs. If you want to go see them, you prepare some coca to go give them as an offering. When you come to them, you say to them:
– Hello. Are you okay grandfathers?
– Yes, as you can see, grandson. Then they show you a seat to sit on. And they offer you a meal of cassava bread with manioc sauce, and manioc beer. This food must not be eaten. It is reserved for the forest masters. If you eat it, you are immediately affected. This could take away your soul, to keep it permanently at their home. You answer:
– I have already eaten, grandfather.
– Well, grandson. Then you return to sit with them. They then offer coca. Always the same: you just pretend to take their coca. When they blow the snuff, you don't inhale it. And you don't

smoke their cigar either. Then they tell us myths. Their roundhouse is so resplendent that it gives hallucinations just to look at it. Many things are painted with stripes. The big central pillars are painted this way. Are also painted: the peripheral pillars, the calabashes, the calabash holders, the seats, the clubs, the spears, the pots. All the things that are inside the roundhouse are painted. That's why when tapirs inflict an infection on a child, and the soul of the child ends up at their home, he has visions that make him see all colors. Then you say:

– Grandfathers, as I came to get something, I give you this offering of coca. And you offer it to them. They say then:

– That's good, my grandson. What are you coming for?

– I came because I would like you to explain to me how your shamanic things are.

– Well, my grandson. Now that you have made this offering to us, we will teach you the origin of our things. One of the weapons that we received is an arrow with jaguar spirit. With this, we punish the people who harm us, or cut down our fruit trees. Thus the spirit of this arrow stands under our trees. As for our spears, they have the spirit of thunder. When some people come to bother us in our bathing river, we kill them with a flash of lightning. Because our children can't even fetch water. It's our way of keeping intruders away. And if we don't want to frighten them, children can also go there in the form of bats or moth, to take water and swim. The wind can also be called to make them fall from above. That way, they will not come fetch water anymore. That's what tapirs tell us.

Shamans have also visions that allow them to enter the world of tapirs and interact with them. Here again it is necessary to avoid falling into traps by dodging all that is offered immediately by the masters, and even to avoid looking at the fascinating colorful patterns of their house. At first, the newcomer has just to present his offering, and it is only when his request is asked that he can hope to receive some information about it. The weapons of tapirs have a spirit perceived in another form for humans.

The forest masters take different forms to eat fruits that affect children.

In the world of these, the arrows of tapirs are jaguars, and their spears strike like lightning. The children of tapirs can also hide themselves in the form of bats or moths.

The weapons of deers

The brocket deers also live like humans, and have lots of weapons to inflict ills and fainting. Their arrows contaminate the fruits, and this can affect the children. You can also go see them. You prepare offerings of coca, snuff and cigar. Once arrived at their home, you say:

– Are you okay, grandfather?

– Yes. As you see, my grandson. It's good to have the opportunity to see each other.

They show you a bench to sit. They offer a cassava with manioc sauce, and manioc beer. You must not swallow anything they give us. Then you return to sit on your seat. They offer us some coca, and blow snuff. But you can't absorb anything.

You chew only your own coca, because theirs could harm you. Then you say to them:
"I came to ask you something, grandfathers. I haven't come empty-handed, I brought you an offering.
And you give them the coca you have brought. They say: "Well, my grandson. We accept this coca of elders." Then you talk with them about the myths. After a while, you tell them: "So, you live like that, grandfathers. How beautiful here!" Their roundhouse is magnificent. But it is not colored. Only their clothes are red. You ask to them:
- Grandfather. What is the use of this great spear?
- It is our weapon. It is used to hunt, or punish people, when they bother us. It has a snake spirit.
- Well, grandfathers. They say also:
- That's our alcohol of salt lick[27]. In a calabash, the beverage is greenish. And they add: "This alcohol, which we received, is very toxic. When humans come to bother us, we make them drink to poison. Afterwards, they vomit green. We punish them when we are disrespected. They also explain:
- As for this snuff, it is for the children and the women who walk on our grounds, especially those which have their menstruations or who have just given birth. Because they dirty all our things! Then we blow them this snuff which, by spiritual ways, inflicts fainting. And their souls end up to be here. This is how we punish those who don't listen to us. Likewise with this cigar.
If these same people come a little too close, we blow tobacco smoke to them. And their bodies are covered with itchy spots. They give them an unbearable heat. That's how we punish them.
As for those who kill our fruit trees, or kill our pets[28], we capture their souls so that they come to replant our trees, and replace these animals.

---

[27] **Mawai** (Yuc.). *Guarapo de salado* (Ver. Span.). Alcohol that animals like deer and tapirs are supposed to drink in their salt lick (*salado* in Spanish).

We want to be respected by young people." That's why, we, the shamans and the healers, recommend that the children walk only where they know, especially not on the land of the forest masters, and even less without shamanic defense. We often say: "Walk with a good shamanic defense. If you listen to me, nothing bad will happen to you." Brocket deers also explain the power of *chundú*[29]. It belongs to them especially.

The universe of deer is quite similar to that of tapirs, but their houses are not colored. Only the dresses of the red brocket (*Mazama americana*) appear as opposed to the dresses of the gray brocket (*Mazama gouazoubira*). Some deer weapons also have a spirit that emerges in a different form in the world of humans, including spears that affect the latter as snakes. Like the tapirs and the other masters of the forest, the brockets can punish the souls of humans when they annoy them. Once they have been softened by the offerings of the shaman, the brockets reveal to him the secrets of the poisons which they offer at first to every stranger. The salt lick are like swamps in which tapirs, deer and other animals drink water to assimilate the mineral salts essential to their bodies. In their world, tapirs and deer use it as their friendly and festive drink in the same way as alcohol for humans. But such a liquid is highly toxic to the latter. One day Fermín showed me a salt lick in the forest, he told me that he knew a non-believer who tasted it and died of it.

Like most non-humans, tapirs and deer hate the slightest drop of uterine blood, even the smell they detect from afar. This is why women cannot accompany their husbands into the forest when they are menstruating or after giving birth.

If they pass on the lands of these large mammals, they throw them snuff which inflicts them sometimes fatal dizzy spells.

---

[28] According to Fermin, deer have various pets (esp.

[29] **Ñujú** (Yuc.). *Chundú* (Ver. Span.). Power of control over the soul of others, which can, for example, seduce or drive him crazy.Mascotas) such as armadillos and pacas.

They can also blow tobacco smoke that results in itching and unbearable heat. As for humans who fell their fruit trees and kill their pets, they capture their souls to replace them and repair their damage.

Deer also have the reputation of controlling some odorous substances with attractive effects called *chundú*. There are different types, but all have in common to influence the victim to the advantage of the person who uses it. Some ethnic groups, such as the Macuna, are feared for their mastery of *chundú*. Most often, it is used as a love-potion, that is, to magically seduce a woman. After my requests for clarification, Fermín told me that the red and gray brockets have the area between their fingers that turn green when they are killed, and that we must not touch them because we risk of becoming sick, or having nausea, fainting, fever, headache, etc. All these evils are effects of the *chundú*. There are incantations to prevent or heal these evils, as well as the other weapons of the deer and tapirs[30].

---

[30] I transcribed and analyzed these incantations with Milciades.
Cf. Fontaine, 2005.

CONCLUSION

With our investigation of the Yucuna healers, we have discovered their specific learning methods, as well as the range of possibilities specific to their shamanism. First of all we have seen that shamanism is not as threatened as it seems, long after the last shamans of a lineage or an ethnic group disappeared. At any time, their shamanism can be recovered, rehabilitated and redeveloped by one of their descendants, provided that he respects the prescriptions of a competent shaman trainer, regardless of his ethnicity, the time necessary for the assimilation of teachings and mastery of the ancestors' powers.

Since time immemorial, the Yucuna shamans have been able to test and benefit from a learning secret that we are still far from having understood or being able to implement in the industrialized societies. The basic rule is to fast or diet to better receive the words and powers of spirits, human or non-human ancestors. The diet deep cleans the body of the apprentice, which has two main types of advantage. On the one hand, it makes him disappear completely from the field of detection – or attraction – of enemies and predators (visible or invisible) which, from then on, have no more possibility or desire to attack him or to inflict diseases. On the other hand, the diet puts the whole of the physical and psychic capacities of the apprentice at its optimum level, in particular to support very harmful substances like the yagé[31], or the weapons and mantles of the spirits of the forest.

---

[31] Some studies in Russia (sanatorium de Goriachinsk) and in Germany (Buchinger method) have shown that fasting heals many diseases. More recently, several studies of Valter Longo from the Californian University of Los Angeles has shown that fasting for cancer patients not only increases their chances of healing, but also makes them tolerate much larger doses of chemotherapy and thus overcomes the disease more easily.

Another lesson of this study is to explain the power of incantations on entities. Incantations have no effect in themselves, or by the power of the shaman alone. Like all prayers, these words have effects to the extent that they call certain ancestors and spirits who, by listening to them and receiving the offerings they appreciate, allow themselves to be softened to act in the sense of the demands of incantation. And it is by such incantations invoking the shaman ancestors that one can durably transform the body of the apprentice to give him shamanic powers.

Since his earliest childhood, the young man has been prepared by listening daily to myths and extraordinary hunting stories. These have gradually built an essential frame of reference to understand and anticipate the phenomena of its natural environment. But as soon as the apprentice has been marked with genipa dye, to fast and thus develop his shamanic powers, all he has learned acquires a new threshold of reality. His new modes of perception allow him to directly apprehend the hitherto invisible world of non-humans. It is also possible for him to communicate with them and to receive their tools to survive and help other humans. Once he has entered the path of the elders, full of trials and dangers, how could he question the value of his experience? How could he ever doubt for just an instant the reality of spiritual beings encountered by dint of courage and perseverance? Their teachings have not only been learned, they have been experienced in the depths of his body. Then nothing in his perceptivity of the world will ever be like before.

BIBLIOGRAPHY

DESCOLA Philippe, 2013, *Beyond Nature and Culture*. Janet Lloyd (trans.). Chicago: University of Chicago Press.

FONTAINE Laurent, 2011, Les cours d'eau dans les incantations chamaniques des Indiens yucuna (Amazonie colombienne). *Journal de la Société des Américanistes*, n. 97-1, pp. 119-149. https://journals.openedition.org/jsa/11693

FONTAINE Laurent, 2013, De l'agentivité mythique et incantatoire. Le mythe de Kawáirimi chez les Yucuna (Amazonie colombienne). Nanterre. *Ateliers d'anthropologie*, n°39. http://ateliers.revues.org/9481

FONTAINE Laurent, 2014, *La nuit pour apprendre. Le chamanisme nocturne des Yucuna.* Société d'ethnologie. Collection "Anthropologie de la nuit" dirigée par Aurore Monod Becquelin.

FONTAINE Laurent, 2015, Ouvrage de recherche : *Tropes et agentivité dans les incantations des Yucuna d'Amazonie colombienne* (Tome 1), 292 p. ;
Annexe 1 : *Encyclopédie des invocations* (Tome 2), 378 p. ;
Annexe 2 : *Incantations* (Tome 3), 670 p.

FONTAINE Laurent, 2016, L'agentivité métaphorique dans les incantations des Yucuna d'Amazonie colombienne, *Bulletin de l'Institut Français d'Études Andines*, n°45(1), pp. 63-89. https://journals.openedition.org/bifea/7834

FONTAINE Laurent, 2017, Ce qu'on ne dit pas chez les Yucuna. In : *Les ruses de la parole. Dire et sous-entendre. Parler, chanter, écrire.* Micheline Lebarbier (éd.), Karthala.

BIBLIOGRAPHY Continued

JACOPIN Pierre-Yves, 1981, *La parole générative de la mythologie des Indiens Yukuna*. Thesis. Neuchâtel : Université de Neuchâtel.

JACOPIN Pierre-Yves, 1988, On the Syntactic Structure of Myth, or the Yukuna Invention of Speech. *Cultural Anthropology* 3 (2), pp. 131-158.

VIVEIROS DE CASTRO Eduardo, 1996, Cosmological Perspectivism in Amazonia and Elsewhere. Cambridge. University of Cambridge.

REFERENCE STORIES

Stories available on the web page:

http://site.laurentfontaine.free.fr/Narrations.html

MATAPI Mario, 2006, *Mythe du Vautour Pape.*

MATAPI Mario, 2006, *Histoire de Ka'marí.*

RODRÍGUEZ YUCUNA Fermín, 2005, *Mythe de l'homme qui prit une femme vautour pape.*

RODRÍGUEZ YUCUNA Fermín, 2008, Histoire des Je'rúriwa.

YUCUNA Edilberto, 2005, *Histoire de Karupe.*

YUCUNA Milciades, 2007, *Mythe de l'homme qui prit une femme vautour pape.*

Stories available on the web page:

http://site.laurentfontaine.free.fr/Savoirs_chamaniques.html

RODRÍGUEZ YUCUNA Fermín, 2006, *Les maîtres des fléaux.*

RODRÍGUEZ YUCUNA Fermín, 2008, *Le chemin des âmes défuntes.*

Hearing Others' Voices

ABOUT HEARING OTHERS' VOICES

A transcultural and interdisciplinary series edited by anthropologist Ruth Finnegan and others for Callender Press, to inform and engage general readers, under-graduates and, above all, young adults and students to reflect on who and where they are and to explore recent advances in thought, unaccountably overlooked areas of the world, and contemporary key issues.

Each volume is by an acknowledged expert (international authority, fellow of a national academy, professor, or the like, together with the brightest of younger scholars and practitioners) – authors who are eager to communicate outside the too often closed realms of academe. General readers will find much to interest them, set out in straightforward but not simplistic terms. But it is above all to the eager young that the series is directed – the generation who will soon hold our precious earth and its resources and peoples in their hands and be responsible for it.

Less textbooks, more exciting collections for reflection and challenge, the series gives readers a unique route into greater awareness of our wonderful world, far and near, east and west, past and present.

 The series logo was created specially for us by the celebrated designer Rob Janoff, creator of the Apple logo, hopefully a feature that will play well with a young adult computer-mad audience.

The first volumes were released in November 2018, preceded by the October launching Chengdu, west China of the Chinese version of Rob Janoff's amazing personal account of how he created the famous apple logo.

Hearing Others' Voices

JOIN THE HEARING OTHERS' VOICES COMMUNITY

Welcome. I look forward to receiving your ideas, questions, arguments, criticisms and challenges. Let's hear your views, read your poems and see your art and other materials. Photos and videos too, images, and links to music and poetry and thoughts please, your own and others'.

The series, after all, is called **Hearing Others' Voices** – yours very much included – so that's what it's all about.

Ruth f

ruthhfinnegan.com

RUTH FINNEGAN
OBE FBA FAFS FRAI

Emeritus Professor
The Open University

Anthropologist and
prize winning author

www.hearingothersvoices.org

callenderpress.co.uk

callendervision.org

Why not join the Oak Grove Readers and Writers Association on Facebook and get the FREE eBook LISTEN TO THIS.

Callender Press

Lightning Source UK Ltd.
Milton Keynes UK
UKHW050326140123
415281UK00011B/163